By David King and Jim Starkey

HIGH
PERFORMANCE
INTERVIEWING

A Compact Concepts Publication.
Compact Concepts is a trademark of Compact Concepts LLC.
The Diamond Circle Logo is a trademark of Compact Concepts LLC.
The CC Infinity Logo is a trademark of Compact Concepts LLC.

Copyright © David King and Jim Starkey 2012.

All rights reserved.

This publication may not be reproduced in whole or in part by any means whatsoever without written permission from the authors.

Compact Concepts
763 W. Happfield Drive
Arlington Heights, IL 60004
USA

Customer service: info@compactconcepts.com
www.compactconcepts.com

Published By: Aleo Publications, Division of P.F.C. Supply Co. Inc.
www.aleopublications.com
P.O. Box 1085
Dundee, IL 60118

Printed in the USA

ISBN # 978-0-9856081-2-5
Library of Congress Control Number: 2012943197

High Performance Interviewing is the first in a series of Compact Concepts publications.

Compact Concepts are high-density books designed for executives who want to read fast, learn fast, and get to the point.

CONTENTS

INTRODUCTION 3

THE CONCEPTS

  1. ANTICIPATE 5

  2. DEFINE YOURSELF 17

  3. TAKE CONTROL 27

  4. BUILD YOUR VISION 39

  5. STRUCTURE YOUR INFORMATION 49

  6. REVEAL YOUR PASSION 59

  7. FINISH STRONG 69

FINAL THOUGHTS 80

INTRODUCTION

Interviews have the power to change your life. A strong interview performance at the right time puts your career onto a new trajectory – a more senior executive level, a geographical move, a novel direction.

High Performance Interviewing is designed to make you better than your competition. It empowers you to take control of an interview and deliver the messages that matter in the most effective way. It offers a strategic perspective on interviewing, from the preparation, through the meeting, all the way to the follow-up, providing insights and techniques for communicating your value to a prospective employer in the limited time available.

We have presented our material in a format we call compact concepts. The seven concepts can be read and assimilated rapidly. Summaries at the end of each chapter are ideal for refreshing your memory. Application of any of the concepts will improve your interview performance. Combining them will give you a step change.

High Performance Interviewing is not intended to provide a template to be rigidly applied in every interview scenario, nor does it seek to list all possible interview questions and propose answers. Rather, it is a toolbox that provides the skill sets necessary to navigate and capitalize on any interview situation.

While this book was written for senior executives and senior executive aspirants, the concepts are pertinent to any job interview scenario. They can be applied with success by students or by CEOs. They are effective for all styles of interviewing – phone, video conference, or face-to-face.

In today's time-pressed world, the majority of interview performances, even at the most senior levels, are well below candidates' true potential. We encourage you to use this book to raise your interview performance and accelerate your career.

Anticipate
1.1 Build Your Foundation
1.2 Visualize
1.3 Create Your Perspective

1. Anticipate

Anticipation is the cornerstone concept of a High Performance Interview. It allows you to leverage the other six concepts and empowers you to access all of your attributes.

Good anticipation makes you smarter by getting your thinking done in advance. It enables you to pre-empt questions and buys you time when you need it most. Further, it gets you into the right frame of mind, makes the interview feel familiar, and helps you to relax and focus.

Anticipation however requires some effort. It is more than just research. It is the act of building on your research with thinking and rehearsal, conditioning yourself to envision how the interview might develop, and planning how you will respond to anticipated questions from the interviewer.

1.1 Build Your Foundation

Regardless of your seniority or experience, build a foundation of knowledge and thought for every interview. Don't put yourself at a disadvantage by being too casual.

Know what you want. Successful people have direction. You should always know why you are attending an interview, where it fits into your career plan, and what you want to achieve. Sometimes you will be exploring, but if you are, then at least know that you are exploring and what you are seeking to find out. Be sure that you are committed to doing a High Performance Interview. A lack of commitment leads to a lack of preparation, a poor result, and disappointment. Don't waste precious time. If you don't feel committed, then disengage.

Do your research. The accessibility of information through the Internet and other sources means you can do solid research for any interview quickly. The obvious first steps include reading the job specification, reading the company website, understanding the company's value proposition and products, and studying competing companies. Next you will want to read commentary from people outside of the company. Seek out articles from a combination of financial or industry analysts from trade publications or mainstream media, and find a good third-party industry report. Also be sure to learn what you can about the key people from the company website, LinkedIn, Facebook, or elsewhere. All of these sources will help you to build a picture of the company and its culture.

Do your thinking. Doing the reading is just a start. You need to develop your own views on the company and the industry. What are the themes running through the business at this time in their lifecycle? What are their pain points and what are the pain points of their customers? What are the most vexing problems confronting them? What is the next milestone in the development of the business? What does this mean for the position you're applying for? You may not be correct in all of your analysis, but the act of thinking independently will ensure you have developed a well-articulated opinion you can discuss and that you have good questions to ask.

Make an assessment. When you have learned all you can with the time and information available, and you have done your thinking, ask what this means for you. How well do you qualify? Are you in a strong or weak position? What do you like and dislike? Is this company in a good position? Does its position make sense for you? Does it excite you? What does this tell you with regard to your preparations; do you need to do additional study? Are there people who can give you more insight or offer you valuable advice?

1.2 Visualize

Visualization is commonly used by athletes but seldom by executives. Our performance arena is the meeting room. Rather than physical prowess, it is our ability to master the conversation that separates winners from losers. Visualize how conversations will progress, and you will be ready to capitalize as the dialogue develops.

Imagine the interview. Envision the type of interview you will be attending. If it is a long session with an executive search firm, you can expect a detailed investigation of your history. If it's a thirty-minute phone call with the company chairman, it's more likely a discussion of your current skills and opinions as applicable to the role. Think about the different stages of the interview, and imagine the likely questions you'll be asked. In all likelihood, you won't be far off. Your own list of questions doesn't need to be long because your focus is not on the questions but on the content of your answers. You will build your content as you work through the concepts in this book, and you'll see your answers becoming sharper and richer.

Mentally Rehearse. See yourself delivering the answers you have prepared. Don't just think them through in your mind; actually say the words out loud so that they feel familiar. With experimentation you will find more powerful and more memorable word combinations (See 2.3 Create Your Messages). Ideally you should feel a certain resonance in the answers that you prepare. They should give you a lift, enabling you to build momentum as the meeting progresses.

You are not aiming to repeat verbatim what you have said in your mental rehearsals. If you do this, you will sound over-rehearsed and wooden. The thought process, however, will make your performance more fluent. It will be easier for you to reproduce your ideas using the questions you're asked to your advantage (See 3.2 Leverage the Questions). Imagine yourself providing both strong content and a poised delivery.

1.3 Create Your Perspective

Successful people have the ability to create their own perspective. They see reality in a positive light and leverage this perspective to achieve more.

Set your expectations. People rarely perform beyond their own expectations. Before working through all seven concepts in this book, set yourself an expectation of success. See yourself delivering a High Performance Interview long before it happens. A useful technique is to list previous successes. This could include career achievements, presentations, negotiations, management challenges solved, and previous interviews. Recall the details of the situations, what you did, how you felt, and why you triumphed. From this positive perspective, make a list of your qualifications for the role in question and reasons why you should be successful with this interview. Expect to succeed.

Set your objectives. Most interviews will follow a pattern: an introduction, an exploration of your history, a discussion of the role and its challenges, an opportunity for you to ask questions, and a conclusion. Depending on the type of position, there may also be a case study or situational questions. Knowing this in advance, you can plan for each section of the interview. Think about each segment; determine what you want to achieve and the messages you want to deliver during that portion of the interview. Clear objectives drive a higher performance.

Get organized. Confidence doesn't only come from within ourselves. Confidence is accumulated by doing the right things and by being with the right people. The assessment you made when building your foundation will highlight actions you should take. Plan these actions into your schedule between now and the interview so you are prepared and so you feel prepared.

These actions might include desk research, meeting knowledgeable intermediaries, talking to friends or colleagues, and even planning your travel arrangements. Focus on the task. Don't imagine you are the only person serious about getting this job.

Anticipate Examples

EXAMPLE 1

From David King: After some years of consulting, I was invited to interview at a more prestigious firm and was excited about the prospect of working there. I came through two rounds of interviews and was back for the third round, meeting some more senior consultants. At the time I was consulting to a mobile phone manufacturer. Early in the interview, I was asked about the mobile industry's broader dynamics and catalysts in the growth of the market. I gave a poor answer, my thoughts being limited to the phone manufacturer's perspective with which I was most familiar. I wasn't ready to discuss the bigger picture with any confidence. By the very next day, my head was full of ideas about the mobile industry. I had enough raw material to give a great answer to this question, and within twenty-four hours, my subconscious was serving me up profound insights. Unfortunately I had not put enough effort into building my foundation and visualizing. If I had done so, all of the ideas that arrived in my head would have been readily available on time for the interview and not one day later.

EXAMPLE 2

From Jim Starkey: I was invited to interview for a senior sales role at a good engineering firm. My sales background is not strong. I am a marketing executive. But I took it very seriously, built a good foundation of knowledge, and prepared good answers to compensate for my lack of sales experience. I came second in that selection process. At the time I was disappointed, but just a few months later they reconnected with me and, after further interviews, offered me the senior marketing position in the company. They had a good impression of me following my previous preparation and my positive approach. They came straight back to me when the right opportunity presented itself.

EXAMPLE 3

From David King: Some years ago, one of my subordinates was meeting with the company's CEO to discuss an internal promotion. I knew the boss well, so I advised the candidate that the CEO would not have had time to think much about the interview and would probably open with a simple "How are you?" At this point the candidate shouldn't say simply that he is well. He should take advantage of the opening and say, "I'm great – I'm sure you are aware that my team has had a very successful quarter and that we are fifteen percent ahead of our quota." The meeting started exactly as I had anticipated. The candidate, buoyed by a strong opening, gained momentum as the meeting progressed and was awarded the promotion.

Anticipate Point Summary

Build Your Foundation

- Know what you want
- Do your research
- Do your thinking
- Make an assessment

Visualize

- Imagine the stages of the interview
- Mentally rehearse

Create Your Perspective

- Set your expectation
- Set your objectives
- Get organized

Define Yourself

2.1 Know Your Story
2.2 Determine Your Strategy
2.3 Create Your Messages

2. Define Yourself

It is not uncommon to come away from an interview feeling like the interviewer never got to know you. This is not a failing on the interviewer's part. One characteristic of high performance candidates is that they make it their responsibility to convey exactly who they are and why they are special, in the limited time available.

In order to show an interviewer what you will be able to do for him or her, you must define yourself. Know exactly who you are, why you are valuable, and how you can best communicate this.

Candidates who take the time to define themselves thoroughly build critical self-awareness that will benefit both their interview and their career going forward. Thorough self-definition forces you to think about how you are different, why that difference is important, and how you can describe your advantages as economically but also as powerfully as possible. It is not a trivial task. If it doesn't feel like hard work, you are probably not being thorough enough.

2.1 Know Your Story

If you cannot find what sets you apart from other candidates, it is unlikely an interviewer will.

Assemble your data. Formulate information regarding your history into a structure. Here is one format you might use:

- Strengths – What am I good at, compared with my peer group?
- Weaknesses – What am I not so good at, compared with my peer group?
- Experience – What have I done and what have I achieved?
- Learning – What have I learned from all of the above?
- Values – What do I care about and what am I looking for?

Don't restrict your experience and learning to a list of job titles. Identify multiple events that happened over the relevant time periods: deals negotiated, projects completed, relationships built, and arguments won or lost. Note what you gained from all of these.

In addition to your own analysis, complement your knowledge with other inputs. If you have been subject to 360-degree feedback in previous jobs, draw on comments from colleagues, superiors, and subordinates. Ask close colleagues or friends for feedback and observations. Learn from a variety of online personality tests.

Become self-aware. Examine your discoveries. Interviewers will be more interested in your recent history than your distant past, but when building self-awareness, it helps to go some way back and walk through your history in detail. You will identify patterns that provide insight and themes that indicate strengths or vulnerabilities.

Look a layer down in the detail to understand not only what you are good at, but why. Identify your differentiators, and the combinations of differentiators that give you your uniqueness. This level of self-awareness is essential if you are going to compete in a field of well-qualified candidates.

Ask yourself multiple questions: What environments work for you? What do people say you are good at? Do you work well with colleagues, or do you get things done by being the master of conflict? What important decisions have you made, and how did things play out? Dig into your answers and determine what this tells you.

Be aware that your weaknesses are likely your strengths being overplayed. Looking at yourself from this perspective often sheds light on adjustments you can make to capitalize on your strengths and also ways to frame your learning and experience from a positive perspective.

Keep a learning log. Make notes regarding your findings. Refer to them and build on them periodically. This will save you the time of recreating all your thoughts every time you need to do this analysis. There is no real end to this process. Our characters unfurl as we get older and as we are confronted with different situations. Be conscientious about working on your learning log after each major career experience while details are still vivid in your mind.

Approach "your story" in a focused and structured way. Give it the time it deserves, and you will come to know how to leverage both your story and yourself. Without a deep understanding of your story, it is hard to progress to Your Strategy (2.2) and Your Message (2.3).

2.2 Determine Your Strategy

Interviews are competitive. High performance interviewees have a strategy for how they intend to win.

Identify the winning criteria. Interviews are driven by "business pain." Businesses hire executives to solve problems and take advantage of latent opportunities. Your first step in defining the winning criteria is understanding the pain. As with "Know Your Story," don't be superficial. Go a level down in the detail. It is not enough to know that "growth has been slower." You need to know why growth is slower, or at least have strong hypotheses. Don't stop at the pain of the company. Think about the industry, the customers, and competitors. Think about key individuals in the company and what they will need from the newly hired executive.

Use your research and pain analysis to list all the criteria that matter. Divide your list into qualifiers and winners. Qualifiers are the criteria a candidate must meet in order to be seriously considered. Winners are the criteria you believe will separate the selected candidate from the others on the short list. Role descriptions supply some of this information, but independent thought is required to give you additional insight. Use your imagination to answer the questions, "What type of candidate would truly exceed their expectations?" and "What does the best imaginable candidate look like?"

Plan your attack. Determine how you intend to win. Look at yourself from multiple perspectives – personality, experience, contact network – and seek out ways to match your assets with the winning criteria. It is unlikely one skill alone will suffice. That is not the nature of executive roles. It will be a portfolio that wins you the job. As you do this, look for combinations of your assets that together make you unique. If your differentiators can be matched by most other candidates, you have not yet found the answer. Be creative, and think about soft skills as much as hard facts.

Check if you meet all the qualifying criteria. You should meet most of these items. It's all right if you're missing a few, because executive search firms typically write long wish lists. If you have gaps, look to your learning and experience to identify how you compensate for missing elements, and decide how you will address this in the meeting. Don't be put off by this situation. Rarely do senior executive candidates have everything on the list.

If you are doing longer-term career planning and aren't currently in an interview process, you have the time to build winners into your portfolio of assets. This is important. High performance candidates keep looking ahead, asking themselves what experience they will need to differentiate themselves in the future. Then they set goals and strategies to obtain that experience.

2.3 Create Your Messages

Interviews are conversations. Your strategy will be executed by creating key messages you can package and weave into the conversation.

Develop your sound bites. When you have devised a winning strategy, put it into words. Write down the key messages you want to deliver. An hour-long interview presents multiple opportunities to convey the messages that matter, so prepare a good number, perhaps fifteen to twenty messages. Don't feel restricted by the number. Think about different types of messages. Some will be about your experience and achievements, others perhaps about your style and values. Read through your messages. Be sure that you cover the qualifying criteria, but more importantly, articulate why your particular skill combination sets you apart from other candidates. Communicate your unique value. You need to stand out as different.

Make your messages meaningful, and keep them simple. Remember the pain analysis you did and the ideas you've had regarding the winning criteria. Be sure that your messages are personalized to address their pain. You need to be relevant. This may mean slight adjustments as you meet different people in the corporation.

Construct short sentences. Nobody remembers long, involved passages. Avoid clichés, jargon, and sounding trite. Edit any clutter from your statements, and get to the point.

Prioritize. Group your messages and create a hierarchy. The highest-priority messages will be fundamental to your strategy; the others will build out the picture. Read over your messages several times. The more familiar you are with them, the easier it will be to include them in your conversation.

Even when an executive or recruiter does a full day of interviewing, or when several people interview the candidates and it takes days for them to compare notes, high performance interviewees are memorable. They achieve this distinction by creating and delivering a clear, powerful set of messages built around their strategy. Time spent sharpening your messages will make the difference between being remembered and being forgotten.

Define Yourself Examples

EXAMPLE 1

From David King: I interviewed an MBA student at Wharton who had been a journalist prior to his postgraduate studies. I asked him what makes a good journalist. He replied, "You have to know when to execute. If you write too early, you risk being wrong. If you write too late, or not at all, you're not a journalist; you're just a talking shop." It was a great sound bite. I have remembered it for thirteen years. It displayed a certain judgement, decisiveness, and courage in addition to strong communication skills – all in a couple of sentences.

EXAMPLE 2

From Jim Starkey: I met with a young candidate for a technical marketing positioning. Early in the interview, he said, "I understand technology, but what I really value is relationships, and that enables me to get things done." It was a good combination, and he managed to emphasize it, without sounding repetitive, a few times during the interview. When he left, his mantra stayed with me.

EXAMPLE 3

From David King: I was recruiting a vice president to lead the management of one of our largest global accounts. I had been introduced to a very experienced guy who had managed this account in the past for another company. He said to me simply, "I can get access to whomever we need to speak to in the account, regardless of their seniority. And before I join you, I'll meet with them to see what they think of your product." It was a simple but clear message that summed up his personal value proposition to me, and it was spoken with such confidence that I knew we had found the right person.

Define Yourself Point Summary

Know Your Story

- Assemble your data
- Become self-aware
- Keep a learning log

Determine Your Strategy

- Identify the winning criteria
- Plan your attack

Create Your Messages

- Develop your sound bites
- Make them meaningful; keep them simple
- Prioritize

Take Control

- 3.1 Get Serious
- 3.2 Leverage the Questions
- 3.3 Build Momentum

3. Take Control

Good chess players don't lose pieces. They decide when they are going to trade them for their opponent's pieces or a sought-after position on the board. In the same way, High Performance Interview candidates do not let themselves become victims of the questions that interviewers pose. They find a way to tell their story.

Taking control is at the heart of a High Performance Interview, and indeed many business meetings. It is a pivotal concept. It does not suggest steamrolling a conversation, but it does mean being acutely aware of the dialogue flow and the messages you want to deliver, then delivering them when opportunities arise.

Candidates who learn to take control never leave an interview wishing they had been asked a different set of questions, or feeling like they left a lot of important material unsaid. They see themselves as responsible for the course of the conversation and act accordingly.

3.1 Get Serious

High Performance Interviewing requires attention to detail. Set yourself high standards, and engage seriously with both the selection process and the interviewer.

Play the part. Be aware that the selectors will have a certain image of what they are looking for. It will vary enormously with position, industry, geography, and culture, but give this the thought it requires for your target position. How should you look, how should you act, and how should you communicate such that you can best be imagined in the role? You are not seeking to create any pretense, but don't put yourself at a disadvantage by acting out of character through a lapse in concentration.

Set the tone. Get a good start. If the interviewer is not quite ready, just wait. Don't be tempted to be drawn into discussion before the interview has begun. An untidy start can throw you off-balance. Similarly, avoid getting drawn into casual sidebar conversations. They can feel comfortable, but they waste time. There is no harm in exchanging a few pleasantries or making reference to a mutual acquaintance, but keep it short.

Have a firm handshake, and make good eye contact. A useful technique is to ask yourself "What color are their eyes?" as it forces you to engage properly. Don't be afraid to refer to your interviewers by name.

Plan well so you are on time and unstressed. Hurried candidates do not appear to be in control. If the interview is via video conference, be sure to arrive early so the equipment can be checked. If video conference or phone connection is lost during an interview, stay calm and wait to be reconnected.

Focus. Remind yourself of the sporting analogy. Successful athletes have the ability to maintain their focus for long periods of time. They are masters of distraction control. When the win/loss margin is narrow, the candidate who has been able to stay focused, not just answering but capitalizing on each question or discussion topic, will emerge the victor. Remove any potential distractions, turn off your phone, and consciously take control of your thinking from the outset.

3.2 Leverage the Questions

Use the interview to your best advantage. Leverage every question to its fullest.

Seize opportunities to deliver value. Every question or piece of dialogue is an opportunity. Listen and detect the openings. Often they come easily, as when the interviewer asks you to "talk through your history" or tell "what can you bring to this role." At other times, the questions can seem narrow, making it a challenge to get to some of your important material (Example: "Why did you find your last boss difficult?") On still other occasions, the questions are so broad that it's easy to answer too generally, missing the chance to insert important details (Example: "Tell me about yourself.")

Consciously deliver value in every answer. Regardless of the question, you need to say something that adds value to your candidature. See your key messages as units of value, and deliver one or two units every time you speak. Don't waste any interview time with moderate or value-neutral answers.

When you visualize (1.2), practice weaving value into your answers. Get familiar with the words you'll use so it's easy to slot a powerful sound bite into a conversation when the opportunity arises. This takes practice and forethought, because you don't know how the questions will be asked.

Bridge (if you need to). A well-known media-interview technique is to bridge from one subject to another. Politicians give great displays of bridging, often ignoring the original question entirely. We are not suggesting you go this far, but bridging is a very useful technique allowing you to expand an answer, refer to particular achievements, or take the conversation in a new direction. As you start each answer, be clear in your mind where you want to take it and if you need to bridge.

Showcase your skills. In addition to your answers to their questions, interviewers will be assessing several other attributes: your analytical skills, communication skills, business acumen, sense of humor, moral courage, charisma, and more. The questions you're asked are not only opportunities for you to deliver your messages but a chance to demonstrate your broader skills. Be aware of this with every answer.

Describe your thought process, so they see that you think clearly. Speak with clarity and authority, so they notice your poise. Don't be afraid to recount mistakes, so they see that you learn. Tell them what you care about, so they observe your energy (Concept 6: Reveal Your Passion).

Work hard with the first two concepts, Anticipate and Define Yourself, and leveraging the questions will come naturally. The openings will seem obvious.

3.3 Build Momentum

Build momentum as the interview progresses. Move the dialogue forward from being a review of your history to a discussion about the challenges.

Keep moving forward. Think of the interview as if it were a presentation. While an interview is clearly a conversation and needs to include give-and-take between you and the interviewer, a presentation perspective is still useful here. You need a strong start, a good theme (Your Strategy), vivid examples, and a strong finish. Presentations have a habit of losing momentum about two-thirds of the way through and need to regain pace before the end. Interviews can do the same, especially if you get mired in talking about your history. Be aware of the potential energy dip (it tends to occur about forty minutes in on an hour interview), and push through it. Use conversational language, don't disappear down tangents, and don't let your answers run too long.

You are less likely to lose pace if you're clear on your target messages, know where you are in the process of delivering them, and move the interview into a discussion of the position's challenges rather than sticking with your history. Interviewers will certainly stay more engaged if you are producing ideas concerning problems they need to solve.

Don't let your guard down. A long interview, and particularly a long day of interviews, is tiring. If you see several people in the same company, you can find yourself repeating answers and possibly telling the same stories a number of times in the same day. You can become quite bored listening to yourself.

Toward the end of such a day, it's easy for a lapse in concentration or energy to derail your performance. Be aware that this is a challenge, and don't let it happen. Remind yourself to work hard and concentrate through every interview. Think of it as a performance. It is your responsibility to be at your best for everyone you meet. No excuses.

Take Control Examples

EXAMPLE 1

From David King: I was interviewing a potential general manager to run the Latin American division of a global software company. There were five candidates. We had intended just four, but the executive search firm found one more, a rising local star they thought we should add to the mix. I asked the young star what he knew about us – opening the way for him to share views on our industry, strategy, and customer base. Instead he said he didn't really know anything, he just came because the search firm invited him. He had landed in the running for a large-scale position that could have accelerated his career ten years, but he wasn't ready and just wasn't serious. He wasted the opportunity.

EXAMPLE 2

From Jim Starkey: I had an interview at a large testing laboratory with the Senior VP of Marketing. I entered the beautiful corner office and had barely introduced myself when another employee came in and began a heated discussion with the person who was to interview me. Within thirty seconds it became the business equivalent of a street fight. I stood there in slight shock, adding to the discomfort with my presence. When the employee stormed out indicating that they would address this later, the VP started the interview. I was uncomfortable and off my rhythm. I should have excused myself when the argument began. I had failed to take control of the situation.

EXAMPLE 3

From David King: Shortly after I took over a global sales leadership appointment, one of my team, the head of sales operations, resigned. I found myself searching for a replacement and trying to define the role at the same time. I met a strong candidate, and told him early in the conversation that I was still thinking about the responsibilities and what the position would entail. Rather than being concerned that the position was a little nebulous, he straightaway entered into shaping the role with me. He took perfect control of the situation, offering several suggestions during the meeting and following up with written ideas later.

Take Control Point Summary

Get Serious

- Play the part
- Set the tone
- Focus

Leverage the Questions

- Seize opportunities to deliver value
- Bridge if you need to
- Showcase your skills

Build Momentum

- Keep moving forward
- Don't let your guard down

Build Your Vision

4.1 Demonstrate Insight
4.2 Articulate Plans

4. Build Your Vision

Interviewers are interested in your history because past performance is usually a fair predictor of future performance. If, however, your interview focuses solely or primarily on the past, then you are leaving the interviewer to do all of the work of envisioning how you would address the challenges that will need to be confronted in the new role.

A High Performance Interview must be future-oriented. The interviewer should see how you think about the challenges, how you plan to get started, what initiatives you are imagining, how you will work with your boss and colleagues, and the studied consideration you've given to pitfalls you may meet along the way.

At the end of an interview, you should have built your vision into the mind of the interviewer to the point where he or she already has a mental image of you working and succeeding in the target position.

4.1 Demonstrate Insight

Build your vision from the outset. Find subtle ways to demonstrate insight into the new role during every stage of the interview.

Seek relevance. In the early sections of an interview where you are likely describing your history, focus on those aspects that are most relevant to the new role. When talking about your achievements, don't necessarily pick the biggest, your favorite, or the most recent. Choose those that will resonate most with the interviewer's needs. Look for opportunities in your answers to find implications regarding your suitability for the target role. Make linkages, explicit or implicit, between what you have done, qualities you have demonstrated, and the demands that will be placed on you in the future.

Be specific. The more specific you can be with your answers, the more credible you will sound. Use the names of real customers and competitors. Go one layer down in the detail whenever possible. Don't talk generically about "taking a look at the organization structure" or "learning about the customer base." Say precisely what you will do, or at least what hypotheses you will test; "I will look at moving to a tiered account structure for the sales organization…," "I will investigate upselling the new product to …." Specificity demonstrates preparation, application, and confidence.

Express opinions. The best interviews feel like conversations. The interviewers become engaged by the candidate's ideas, and they discuss them together. You can only do this well if you have built your foundation (See 1.1 Build Your Foundation). Judge how bold you want to be, whether you want to express a strong opinion or pose a question. The more you generate dialogue, the more the interview becomes a discussion between peers rather than a cross-examination.

Demonstrating insight shows you are mentally in tune with the position and that you have already given thought to the challenges. It builds credibility and makes the dialogue real.

4.2 Articulate Plans

Articulating plans moves the dialogue forward, engages the interviewer, and transforms an interview from a question-and-answer session to a future-oriented discussion.

Establish time horizons. Describe your objectives and activities against different time horizons. No one can do everything at once, and you need a way of structuring your thoughts so they are easy to explain and to understand. Typical time periods are: settling in, the first ninety days, the first year, and the long-term. You can be quite specific regarding settling in and the first ninety days and be more visionary about time periods beyond that.

Define milestones. You can make plans more specific by discussing tangible milestones you expect to achieve in each time period. These will doubtless need to be further defined and confirmed after starting in the new role, but in an interview, milestones are useful in a number of ways. They demonstrate how you are thinking. They display your experience, not only in knowing what to do but what resources you'll need and how long it will take. Milestones enable you to test your expectations of what you think you can achieve against the interviewer's expectations for each time period.

Don't be surprised if you get slightly different pictures (from different interviewers) of the same job position. This is not uncommon, and these varying perspectives can be discussed in second or third-round interviews with the direct boss.

Use Your Imagination. Some people feel reluctant to express plans too clearly in case they are mistaken or because they feel they lack information. Don't let these concerns stop you. Be sure to work hard enough with the "Anticipate" concept, and don't be afraid to use your imagination where you are short of data. Your experience from previous jobs will help you. As you gain information with each round of interviews, you can firm up your ideas.

If you're back for a second or third-round meeting, the interviewer expects that you've given thought to your plans. It's a good idea to document your plans and to bring them with you.

Plans are a powerful means of deepening the conversation. You further develop the vision of yourself performing in the role and also get a better understanding of how it would be to work together.

Build Your Vision Examples

EXAMPLE 1

From David King: I needed to appoint a new head of PR. It was not an area I was too familiar with, but it did fit within our marketing department (one of my responsibilities), so after the previous PR manager left, I became embroiled in this search. We had met a number of candidates, and I was relatively happy with them but I didn't know much and wasn't sure. Then we met a new candidate, and everything changed, because she built a vision for me in the interview. In the space of five to seven minutes, she clearly conveyed how I should think about the PR department, what she would do, and how long it would take her to do it. Her approach was so engaging that I remember it well, even though the interview happened years ago. She said, "We are building a narrative here. It is the story of this company over the next three years. You are going to help me to create the story, and I am going to tell you what we need to do quarter by quarter, from a public relations perspective, to make that story the reality in three years' time." As she continued, she was specifically interspersing our product names into her plan, demonstrating clear insight into our business.

EXAMPLE 2

From Jim Starkey: I interviewed for a senior marketing position with a manufacturing company. After a lengthy afternoon with three people, I had a good idea of what I could bring to the table. I studied the company and their products, and when called back for a second interview, I came with a ninety-day plan detailing adjustments I would make to move the organization forward. I qualified my plans with "based on the limited knowledge I have," but they were impressed with the specific expression of opinion, and I was offered the job.

EXAMPLE 3

From David King: I was interviewed for a global sales position. As part of the process, I met with the general manager for China. The very first thing he said as we sat down was, "So what would your sales strategy be?" It was a fair question and a great question. I should have been able to demonstrate my thought process, tell stories, and articulate potential plans. But instead I was taken aback by the speed and directness of his approach, and I stumbled. It would have been different if I had thought about his pain points in advance, visualized a likely start, and prepared my initial hypotheses regarding my plans.

Build Your Vision Point Summary

Demonstrate Insight

- Seek relevance
- Be specific
- Express opinions

Articulate Plans

- Establish time horizons
- Define milestones
- Use your imagination

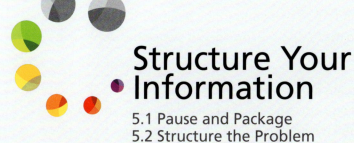

Structure Your Information

5.1 Pause and Package
5.2 Structure the Problem

5. Structure Your Information

Executive search firms typically screen more than fifty candidates for senior positions. They then meet face-to-face with more than twenty candidates. Finally, they put four or five in front of their clients for "first-round" interviews.

The senior executive who is doing the recruiting may try to meet the candidates in quick succession so as to make the comparison easier, but it is more likely in these days of global travel commitments and packed agendas that the interviews will be spread out over several weeks. One of your challenges, in getting through the early cluttered rounds then defeating stiff competition in the later rounds, is to make sure the interviewer remembers what you have said.

You are not expecting this person to remember everything, but you are expecting to make a big enough impact that he or she remembers you, your core messages, the assets you'll bring to the role, and how you differ from the other candidates.

The key to ensuring your message is memorable is to structure your information. If you do that skillfully, you'll deliver more information in a shorter period of time, making it easy for the interviewer to assimilate and recall what you've said.

5.1 Pause and Package

Convey your message clearly and concisely, putting emphasis on the items of most value.

Take your time. Concept 3 (Take Control) explained how you must leverage questions to your own advantage. It is difficult to do this if you hurry. In fact, if you rush to an answer, it's likely you will forget relevant material, lose your way, or lose the interviewer. Avoid this pitfall by taking a second's pause before you begin any answer. Use that pause to decide what you want to include in your answer and how you are going to package the information for best effect. While the pause seems like no time to the interviewer, it is long enough for you to select your material, decide if you want to bridge to another topic, determine where you will start, and – equally important – determine where you will end.

Organize your information. You can choose to package either explicitly ("Let me divide my answer into a few parts") or implicitly (not mentioning the structure but knowing in your mind the topics you will cover). Either way, you will follow a logical flow, avoiding irrelevant material and closing well. There is a certain resonance gained by packaging material in odd numbers of packages (ones, threes, and fives), so think about dividing your material in this way. You probably don't want to say how many pieces of information your answer will contain. It is easy to forget one, and then you are left scrambling.

Be selective. Long answers are not remembered, and worse still, they upset the momentum of a conversation. While it's possible that the interview is a little unbalanced with the interviewee talking more than the interviewer, you still want to aim for a conversation rather than a monologue. Use the pauses to select your salient pieces of information, and don't include more. Clutter is a distraction.

Don't fade out. Think ahead about how you want to conclude your answer so you come to a clean stop and so that it's clear when you've finished. It isn't just the content of answers that matters; the delivery is just as important. Interviewers are looking for tight communicators who can convey a point clearly and easily. A neat finish will add to this effect.

5.2 Structure the Problem

Case studies, situational questions, and open-ended or abstract questions can prove testing. High Performance Interview candidates know how to use a structured thought process and solid principles to unravel even the most complex question.

Put structure to your thoughts. Case studies are sometimes made complicated by the interviewer providing a lot of data that you're left trying to absorb and synthesize. At other times, they're made challenging by a lack of information. In the consulting industry, it is not uncommon to be told something like, "I have a client in the securities safe-keeping industry, but he's losing money," followed by a long pause.

In either situation, don't panic or get tongue-tied. Instead, structure the problem by working through a logical thought process. Build information by asking questions. Use your experience to make explicit assumptions, and start to suggest hypotheses.

You are best doing your thinking out loud, so the interviewer knows where you are going. For example, following the statement above you might say, "I had best understand the cost structure first. Can you tell me more about the fixed and variable costs?" This would get you started and buy you a moment's thinking time while the interviewer is answering. You will collect some data and then move forward again. "So given the high fixed-cost element, can you break that down further for me, into, say, people costs and other costs?"

Make your direction clear and show that there is method behind your questions. Gradually you would establish a picture of cost structure, revenue streams, segmentation, and competitor analysis. Out of this should drop some hypotheses and ideally an answer.

In case studies and situational questions, interviewers can be testing several of your qualifications at once, for example: your analytical ability, lateral thinking, communication skills, and poise. They are not usually concerned about whether you come to a single right answer – it is the approach that matters.

Seek out principles. In addition to following a logical thought process, look for solid principles on which to base your ideas and decisions. This is a powerful way of solving problems.

For example, if you were addressing a complex question about organization design, you might say, "It's always best to organize along the dimension that requires the most expertise. So in this case, where we're dealing with highly differentiated segments, I'd look to set up the business units based on customer segments." If you were asked a question about designing a compensation plan, you might say, "It's important to consider how easy it is to administer the plan, so even if more complexity seems to make strategic sense, it may lead to a lot of queries and delays in compensation being paid."

The advantages of communicating in this fashion are that you demonstrate expertise in the subject matter in addition to a strong rationale for your decision. Most business problems – whether people issues, customer crises, or deal reviews – can be assessed against some solid principle. Seek these out and lean on them when you are being interviewed.

Be creative. When addressing any situational or case study question, challenge yourself to be creative. As explained, you can find the answers to case studies by putting structure to your thought process and/or identifying the principles that matter. Beyond this linear thinking, though, is a more lateral domain that you can access with a little practice.

Always try to look beyond the obvious. Ask yourself if you have had other quite different experiences where there was some valuable learning you can apply to this situation. Try asking yourself a number of "what if" questions. Explore ideas with questions to the interviewer. This is an important time to utilize a positive perspective. You are more likely to be creative if you tell yourself you are creative and set an expectation that you can produce novel ideas.

Structure Your Information Examples

EXAMPLE 1

From David King: I was interviewed via a video conference. The interviewer was late and hurried. Before she had even sat down and was fully on-screen, she said, "So tell me about yourself." It was a vague and untidy start, and sadly I responded in kind with an incoherent answer, still watching to see if she would finally get into her seat and appear on screen. I should have paused to let her get settled, while packaging my information and leveraging the question so I could immediately deliver a number of units of value against the job description at the very start of the interview.

EXAMPLE 2

From Jim Starkey: A candidate contacted me through one of the big social networks, and I arranged an interview for him with a colleague. When I asked my co-worker how it went, he told me he wanted his ninety minutes back! He had asked the interviewee one question, and the candidate had talked for twenty minutes. He asked a second question, and the candidate talked for fifteen more. My colleague was nauseated and wanted the pain to end. The candidate had no rhythm or structure to his answers.

EXAMPLE 3

From David King: I was interviewed by a university professor for a place on his engineering course. He asked, "If I push a football underwater, why does it come up again?" I gave some short answer like, "It has air in it." Painfully, he guided me through a proper reasoning process: "When the ball is under water, what forces are acting on it? (Water pressure all around the ball); What direction are those forces? (Through the center of the ball); What governs the strength of those forces? (Depth). So what does that tell us? (The water pressure pushing up under the ball is higher than the downward pressure at the top). So? (The ball will surface). I should have been looking for the guiding principles.

EXAMPLE 4

From David King: While working for a global consulting firm, I had to attend an assessment for promotion. The assessment entailed exercises, written tests, and interviews. In one of the interviews, I was asked quite a long multi-part question. I knew a lot about the topic, but the complex delivery of the question caused me to go off on a few tangents. This resulted in the piece of my answer that really mattered getting lost in the clutter. When I received feedback the assessor noted that I failed to address the key part of the problem.

Structure Your Information Point Summary

Pause and Package

- Take your time
- Organize your information
- Be selective
- Don't fade out

Structure the Problem

- Put structure to your thoughts
- Seek out principles
- Be creative

Reveal Your Passion

6.1 Engage
6.2 Tell Stories

6. Reveal Your Passion

Organizations run on energy – human energy that comes from their people and from a collective passion to move something forward. Interviewers seek employees or colleagues who will increase the energy quotient of their company.

High Performance Interview candidates reveal their passion so interviewers can feel the energy these candidates will contribute. This does not mean being extrovert, or boisterous, especially if that is not in your nature. It means conveying to the interviewer that you will be generous with your spirit, that you will emotionally engage the task and give it your best, regardless of challenges or setbacks. It means showing the job is something you care about, something that gives you a sense of purpose.

Passion is a powerful tool. Life is full of examples where the human spirit triumphed over insurmountable odds. Everybody knows this, so use your passion to your advantage, and you will raise the level of your performance.

6.1 Engage

High Performance Interview candidates generate energy in interviews. They give the meeting a boost, using nothing more than their personality and their conversation.

Commit to the conversation. Sit up, lean in, and participate from the start. Avoid getting into a listening mode if the interviewer chooses to explain things for you and goes on too long. Look for reasons to interject and contribute.

Create dialogue. Have opinions and ask good questions. Interviewers will nearly always give you the opportunity to ask questions, so think about this in advance and select questions that demonstrate your level of insight, interest, and energy. Don't allow yourself to relax as the interview progresses. Participate fully from beginning to end.

Talk about what you care about. When you leverage the questions (Concept 3: Take Control), look for opportunities to talk about what you care about; what you value doing, what you have succeeded in doing, and what you enjoy doing. Don't be afraid to use humor. You will come across as optimistic, enthusiastic, and high-energy.

As you explore your background, be sure to focus on the positives. It is quite common for interviewers to ask about your weaknesses. Don't be daunted by having to reveal vulnerabilities, disappointments, or mistakes. Draw out the learning and the value of these experiences. Show how this learning is now an asset. As you discuss the position, look forward. Seek out possibilities, share your vision, and generate ideas.

Want the job. Find an opportunity during the interview to tell the interviewer why this position fits with your life plan. Explicitly explain your motivation. There are many potential reasons why the job might be a good personal fit: a natural progression in your career experience, a desired change of industry, a geographical move, or something else.

Also be sure to explain the emotional reasons for why you want the job. Why do you care about this position? There is clearly no single right answer. It will depend entirely on you. But this new job must be something that excites you. There will be plenty of hard days, and the interviewer needs to know you have some inner desire that can keep you going. Be sure that you tell the interviewer why you care, or someone who cares more will outshine you.

6.2 Tell Stories

Stories bring you to life, get you remembered, and reveal your passion. Stories support your claims and provide a window to the real you.

Select your stories. Identify a number of stories from your past that support your interview strategy and illustrate your messages. Try to find about ten so you have a good selection to choose from. Then pick the five or six you feel most comfortable telling and that best reveal the qualifications you wish to exemplify.

Short is good. You will weave a number of stories into the conversation, and the briefer they are, the easier this becomes. Sometimes a few sentences can be enough to make your point, for example a simple example of how you handled a challenging conversation or a phrase you have used when motivating people. Other times you may need something more elaborate: some context, the characters, the actions, and the outcome.

Seek diversity in the stories you prepare. For example, you may want stories that show people skills, customer management, creativity, analytical skills, or resilience.

Plan your delivery. The delivery is as important as the story.

- Be concise. You don't have much time; you can't go on a monologue for too long.

- Be clear. You are seeking effective, memorable means to reinforce your messages; it is critical that the interviewer sees the connections and doesn't get lost.

- Be detailed around the parts that matter most, and especially be specific concerning your contribution. The interviewer wants to know what you did, not just the general run of events. It's sometimes useful to describe what you were thinking, or how you felt at different times of the story, to illustrate your thought process and values.

Mental rehearsal is crucial to good storytelling. Say each story to yourself a couple of times. Think about the structure of the story, check that it flows well, and remove any clutter. Convey the key points as clearly and economically as possible.

Reveal Your Passion Examples

EXAMPLE 1

From David King: The chairman of a company asked me, "How did you spend your time in your last job?" I gave a dull answer regarding X percent here and Y percent there. If I had leveraged the question properly, I would have taken the opportunity to tell him what I liked doing (and hence why that occupied a large percentage of my time). Attacking the question this way would have revealed my passion for certain activities and also focused in on an activity I knew was valuable to him. A small pause at the start, on my part, would have helped me steer the question in a better direction.

EXAMPLE 2

From Jim Starkey: I was asked "What do you do outside of work?" I answered, "I like the outdoors and baseball" – a flat and boring answer. Driving home, I realized I had failed to leverage the opportunity. This was an open-ended question, with no right or wrong answer, where I could have conveyed something of value about myself: my values, energy, diversity, versatility, and more. The next time I was prepared and told a little about my love for kayaking, why it inspired me and I found some ways to relate it to my work. I could tell the interviewer was engaged and learned about my commitment to the things I care about.

EXAMPLE 3

From David King: I interviewed an intern for a consulting firm. He was a young guy with limited experience, but he had spent the previous winter working at a ski resort looking after people's bags when they were out skiing. When he arrived, he discovered it was a real trial finding bags when people came to pick them up. He told a great story about how he designed and implemented a new process. The narration was simple enough, but it was vivid, told with a lot of enthusiasm and showing me his intellect, leadership skills, desire to make things better, and even his sense of humor.

EXAMPLE 4

From David King: After a few years as a management consultant I was interviewing with a larger firm. The interviewer asked me what I had been involved in recently and I mentioned winning a new project for our company. She asked simply "what was your role in this." As it happened, I had an integral role in this win, but I answered simply "well, I wrote the proposal for the project." It was a bland answer completely missing the opportunity for a great story. I should have spoken about the previous project I had delivered, the relationships I had built, the structure I had given to the proposal and how the deal was negotiated – it would have brought me to life and highlighted multiple relevant attributes.

Reveal Your Passion Point Summary

Engage

- Commit to the conversation
- Talk about what you care about
- Want the job

Tell Stories

- Select your stories
- Plan your delivery

Finish Strong

- 7.1 Close Well
- 7.2 Follow-Up
- 7.3 Reflect
- 7.4 Maintain Your Standards

7. Finish Strong

The first six concepts stress the importance of your focus, concentration, and organization. The message from the seventh concept is that you are not finished when the interviewer has asked the last question, or even when you have left the room.

High Performance Interviewing requires working hard beyond the last question, taking time afterwards for a value-adding follow-up, conducting a thorough self-critique, and maintaining the highest professional standards as you do this.

Make a strong finish integral to your interview discipline. A good close and follow-up will make you more memorable. A structured review of the questions and your answers will enable you to sharpen your technique for next time, and high-integrity conduct will safeguard your reputation.

7.1 Close Well

As interviews come to a close, you are often asked if you have any last questions. Take this opportunity to close well, as if you were finishing a presentation.

Summarize. When you have already asked all your questions, use the last prompt for final questions as a cue to take control and make a brief summary. This will give you the opportunity to:

- Reiterate key messages.
- Make explicit linkages between your messages and important topics in the conversation.
- Provide any clarifications you deem necessary.
- Communicate any additional key messages that have gone unsaid so far.
- Confirm your enthusiasm and interest.

Ask about next steps. As the interview closes, remember to ask about next steps in the hiring process. You want to understand what stage they're at in the hiring and their timing. A little information can make for a large reduction in your level of anxiety.

7.2 Follow Up

A follow-up message to an interviewer is an opportunity for an additional interaction.

Send an email to your interviewer(s). It used to be considered polite to send a handwritten physical letter. Nowadays physical letters get lost in the mailroom, so use email, and create a short message that provides the following:

- A repeat of one or two of your key messages – ideally with reference to something discussed in the meeting.

- Something beyond your key messages (something not mentioned in the meeting) that demonstrates an insight you've had into the role since the interview and that further supports your strategy.

- A confirmation of your interest and desire, and any relevant, brief rationale supporting your personal motivation.

Be judicious about whether you send emails to everyone who interviews you. Certainly the hiring manager is important, and generally most people you meet face-to-face. If in the process of interviewing you had phone conferences with other managers or board members, you may decide emails to them are superfluous.

7.3 Reflect

Every time you are interviewed, take a few moments directly afterwards to reflect on your performance and how you could have done better. Continuous improvement will only come through conscious analysis, thought, and practice.

List out what you've learned and plan adjustments. Work through the concepts and make notes.

- Anticipating: Were you well-informed, well-prepared, and ready for the challenge?

- Defining yourself: Did you find a way to differentiate? Was your strategy effective? Did your messages resonate?

- Taking control: Did you engage at the start and stay focused? How well did you leverage the questions? How many of your key messages remained unsaid? Did you build momentum as the interview progressed?

- Building a vision: Were you able to demonstrate insight? Did you articulate any plans demonstrating that you were already thinking about the role?

- Structuring information: Did you pause and package effectively? Did you answer complicated questions with structure and clarity?

- Revealing your passion: How well did you generate energy? Did you select, position, and tell your stories well?

- Finishing strong: Did you take the opportunity to summarize and check the next steps?

Think about your discoveries. You will find some things that you could have done better and at the same time answers where you were very happy with your performance. Record the positive experiences so that you don't forget them. Think about the questions where you feel you should have done better, and decide what you would answer if you had your chance again. Record your new answer. You will always find opportunities to sharpen messages and leverage questions to a greater extent. Time spent thinking about these better prepares you for next time.

Move on. Once an interview is over and you've examined all that you learned, it's time to look forward. It's easy to regret certain answers and feel you missed opportunities, but there's nothing you can change once the interview process is finished. Given that only one person gets the job, there are always more losers than winners in the hiring process. There are also many unknowns regarding other candidates and the personalities of people in the selection process. So don't get upset thinking about "opportunities missed," and don't get depressed if you didn't get the job. The experience of your interview has added to your skills and to your knowledge. Value the interview for all it taught you, and move on to the next one, which is sure to be better.

7.4 Maintain Your Standards

Recognize that every time you go through a recruitment process, you are on display to a broader audience. This can include senior executives, board members, executive search firms, and business acquaintances and colleagues. This is an important time to look after your reputation and maintain the highest standards of integrity.

Withdraw professionally. If you decide to withdraw from a search process, make a phone call to the people concerned and tell them your decision. If you have met or spoken to the hiring executive, be sure to call this person yourself. If you don't get a reply after a few calls, then leave a message so as not to lose time, but be sure to make the effort. If you are at the stage where you have only been dealing with the search firm, then call them (and do it yourself). These people have invested time in you, so they deserve the courtesy of a personal call.

Don't feel you have to explain yourself, you can say simply that the job wasn't right for you at this time. It is much more respectful to tell them this before, rather than after, they offer you the position.

Don't play games with people. It's fine to explore; both sides have to do this. And it's fine to be involved with a few hiring processes at one time; you don't know which one will be successful for you. But once you have decided a position is not for you, demonstrate integrity by taking yourself out of the process.

Be responsive. Once you are involved in a search process, respond professionally to communications you receive. The recruiting world is full of calls and emails that lie unanswered by every party: candidates, search firms, and hiring managers. Rise above this shoddiness and differentiate yourself by always replying promptly. If you need more time to think over a decision, just say so. If you have had a late change of heart, just say so. Take pride in your responsiveness. It will serve you well over time.

Accept rejection gracefully. When you receive a rejection, decide rapidly if you want to explore whether there is anything you can do to get back in the process. Ask for feedback and thank the hiring executive and search firm for the experience. These courtesies cost nothing and foster good relationships for the future.

Tell the truth. The concepts in this book should enable you to identify your best attributes and communicate them effectively. In doing so, be sure you remain honest with yourself and with others. Only you will know if you are in danger of crossing the line from a positive perspective to fabrication, and you can't let that happen.

Finish Strong Examples

EXAMPLE 1

From David King: I was at the end of a very animated interview. Both myself and my interviewer had enjoyed the conversation. There seemed to be good chemistry between us, and we'd shared a number of laughs together during the meeting. As we drew to a close, I was concerned that amidst the laughter he may have missed or forgotten some of my key messages. So I thanked him for a fun discussion but said very clearly, "Before we part, I would just like to reinforce a few key points." He was pleased about the summary and took a few notes, later on offering me the job. My wrap-up may have made the difference between an A versus a B-grade interview.

EXAMPLE 2

From Jim Starkey: I walked a candidate back to my office from an interview he'd just completed with the quality manager. We ran into the president of the company, and I introduced him. The president asked, "Is there anything I can tell you about my company?" The interviewee didn't miss a beat and said, "I have been inspired by my visit today. I'd simply like to know when can I start." It was a good sound bite, well-remembered when he did start. It was also a powerful end note for the day and left us with a strong impression.

EXAMPLE 3

From David King: I was seeking a senior executive to run a global services organization – a crucial hire in the transformation I was driving. I found my target candidate, but he was unsure whether the position was right for him. In order to convince him, I arranged meetings with our CEO and members of the board. Finally he accepted, and I was relieved. Then between his verbal acceptance and the signing of the contract, he had a change of heart and declined the role. He did so by sending me a text message. He was a great candidate, and we had invested a lot of time in him. He had every right to change his mind if the job wasn't for him, but it was careless and thoughtless to decline via text message. We deserved a phone call.

EXAMPLE 4

From Jim Starkey: I interviewed two candidates. They were equal except that one had sent a follow-up message after the interview, and the other one had not. I liked them both, so I brought them each back for a second round so I could compare their responses to my additional queries. I asked the one why he didn't send a follow-up note, and his response was, "I never thought of it." That evening on a major social network, the candidate made light of it: "Oops, guess I'll be writing thank-you notes now!" This was a thoughtless move. It gave the impression that he wasn't taking the position seriously. He should have realized he was still on display.

Finish Strong Point Summary

Close Well

- Summarize
- Ask about next steps

Follow Up

- Send an e-mail to your interviewers

Reflect

- List out what you've learned and plan adjustments
- Move on

Maintain Your Standards

- Withdraw professionally
- Be responsive
- Accept rejection gracefully
- Tell the truth

Final Thoughts

Interviewing is a courting ritual. It is a highly subjective process – an imperfect science – where both sides are provided a small window into the possibilities that might result from merging forces.

The process is complicated by being both competitive and unpredictable. There are many styles of interviews and interviewers, and a wide array of possible questions. As your career progresses, the competition only gets stronger.

Our purpose with this book has been to teach you the skills that win over interviewers. You excel in interviews by communicating your true, full potential and a vision of yourself at your best with respect to the position's and company's challenges. Like any skill, High Performance Interviewing requires work and practice.

Executive careers are effectively an accumulation of experiences: two years here, four years there. The most successful careers are often those that gained access to the most promising opportunities. Key to such opportunities is a candidate's ability to ace the interview.

We wish you success in your hunt for the very best opportunities and encourage your determined ambition and effort in their pursuit. The right interview performance at the right time will change your life.

About the Authors

DAVID KING is chairman of Ascade, a telecom software company, and CEO of Flexenclosure, a company providing renewable energy power solutions to the telecom industry. Based in Stockholm, he has twelve years experience in senior executive roles in European and U.S. high-tech companies. David spent seven years as a strategy consultant and holds an MBA from London Business School.

JIM STARKEY leads the marketing team at OTTO, a North American control-switch manufacturing company. His career spans twenty-five years in engineering and marketing positions at AT&T, Lucent and UTStarcom. He holds a Master of Science degree in Telecommunications from the University of Colorado.

Contact us:
David King at david@compactconcepts.com
Jim Starkey at jim@compactconcepts.com

Learn about other High Performance Interviewing products at **www.compactconcepts.com.**